READ & SPEAK

JAPANESE

FOR BEGINNERS

SECOND EDITION

The Easiest Way to Learn to Communicate Right Away!

Series Concept
Jane Wightwick

Japanese Edition
Helen Bagley • **Jane Wightwick**

New York   Chicago   San Francisco   Lisbon   London   Madrid   Mexico City
Milan   New Delhi   San Juan   Seoul   Singapore   Sydney   Toronto

Copyright © 2011 by g-and-w Publishing. All rights reserved. Printed in the United
States of America. Except as permitted under the United States Copyright Act of 1976,
no part of this publication may be reproduced or distributed in any form or by any
means, or stored in a database or retrieval system, without the prior written permission
of the publisher.

1 2 3 4 5 6 7 8 9 10 11 12 13 14 15 16 17   QDB/QDB   1 9 8 7 6 5 4 3 2 1

ISBN 978-0-07-176646-3 (book and CD package)
MHID   0-07-176646-4 (book and CD package)

ISBN 978-0-07-176647-0 (book)
MHID   0-07-176647-2 (book)

Library of Congress Control Number 2010943204

Other titles in this series

Read & Speak Arabic for Beginners, 2nd Ed.
Read & Speak Chinese for Beginners, 2nd Ed.
Read & Speak Greek for Beginners, 2nd Ed.
Read & Speak Korean for Beginners, 2nd Ed.

McGraw-Hill books are available at special quantity discounts to use as premiums and
sales promotion, or for use in corporate training programs. To contact a representative,
please e-mail us at bulksales@mcgraw-hill.com.

This book is printed on acid-free paper.

Enhanced CD

The accompanying disk contains audio recordings that can be played on a
standard CD player. These recordings are also included in MP3 format. For
iPod or similar player:

1. Insert the disk into your computer
2. Open the disk via My Computer.
3. Drag the folder "MP3 files_Read & Speak Japanese" into the Music
   Library of iTunes.
4. Sync your iPod with iTunes, then locate the files on your player under:
   ARTIST › Read & Speak Japanese for Beginners, 2nd Ed.

Audio Flashcards

The Key Words vocabularies in this book can be studied online in
interactive flashcard format at byki.com./listcentral. Search for "Read and
Speak Japanese" to locate the lists.

CONTENTS

PLUS...

- 8 tear-out cards for fun games

- Audio CD for listening and speaking practice

- Online activities to enhance learning

Read & Speak *JAPANESE*

Welcome to *Read & Speak Japanese*. This program will introduce you to the Japanese language in easy-to-follow steps. The focus is on enjoyment and understanding, on *reading* words rather than writing them yourself. Through activities and games you'll learn how to read and speak basic Japanese in less time than you thought possible.

You'll find these features in your program:

	Key Words	See them written and hear them on the CD to improve your pronunciation.
	Language Focus	Clear, simple explanations of language points to help you build up phrases for yourself.
?	**Activities**	Practice what you have learned through reading, listening, and speaking activities.
	Games	With tear-out components. Challenge yourself or play with a friend. A great, fun way to review.
	Audio CD	Hear the key words and phrases and take part in interactive listening and speaking activities. You'll find the track numbers next to the activities in your book.

If you want to give yourself extra confidence with reading the script, you will find *Your First 100 Words in Japanese* the ideal pre-course companion to this program. *Your First 100 Words in Japanese* introduces the Japanese characters through 100 key everyday words, many of which also feature in *Read & Speak Japanese*.

So now you can take your first steps in Japanese with confidence, enjoyment and a real sense of progress.

Whenever you see the audio CD symbol, you'll find listening and speaking activities on your CD. The symbol shows the track number. Track 1 is an introduction to the sounds of Japanese, including an important feature on Japanese tones. Listen to this before you start and come back to it again at later stages if you need to.

Key Words

2

Look at the script for each key word and try to visualize it, connecting its image to the pronunciation you hear on your CD.

こんにちは	**konnichiwa**	*hello*		*Japanese names:*	
			安紀子 **akiko**		*Akiko (female)*
さようなら	**sayounara**	*goodbye*	優子 **yuuko**		*Yuuko (female)*
			正 **tadashi**		*Tadashi (male)*
... です	... **desu**	*I am ...*	実 **minoru**		*Minoru (male)*

Japanese is written in a combination of three writing systems – *hiragana* and *katakana* alphabets, or "syllabaries," and Chinese characters, known as *kanji*. For example, the greetings in the left-hand column above are written in hiragana, but the names on the right are written in kanji. How a particular word is written depends on the origin of the word and convention.

You will find an overview of the script, including hiragana and katakana tables, in the reference section on page 89, but don't expect to take it all in at once. Concentrate only on the hiragana you need for the three phrases in the Key Words for the moment and build up gradually from there.

Kanji characters offer little clue as to their pronunciation and need to be learned one by one. Look carefully at the characters while listening to the CD, connecting the image to the pronunciation you hear.

How do you say it?

Join the script to the pronunciation, as in the example.

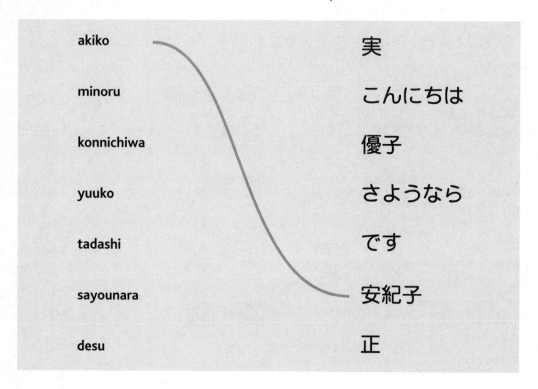

akiko — 安紀子

minoru — 実

konnichiwa — こんにちは

yuuko — 優子

tadashi — 正

sayounara — さようなら

desu — です

What does it mean?

Now say the Japanese out loud and write the English next to each.

こんにちは __hello__   さようなら _____

優子 _____   実 _____

です _____   安紀子 _____

正 _____

Language Focus

To introduce yourself simply say your name, followed by です desu.

安紀子です。   **akiko desu.**
I'm Akiko.

正です。   **tadashi desu.**
I'm Tadashi.

です desu does not change for male or female or the number of people and so also means *he/she is*, *they are*, etc.

When you are addressing someone by name in Japanese you need to add the word さん san after the person's name. This is the equivalent of Mr., Miss, Mrs., and Ms. and is used with both first and last names. It is used much more than its English equivalents. Never use さん san when talking about yourself.

実さん、こんにちは。   **minoru san, konnichiwa.**
Hello, Minoru.

優子さん、さようなら。   **yuuko san, sayounara.**
Goodbye, Yuuko.

The period is written as a small circle in Japanese script: 。

You will notice that Japanese does not have spaces between separate words. This can make reading longer sentences tricky. Try to look for words that you recognize. As you progress through this book you will soon realize that there are lots of words that re-occur, like です desu. Look out for these words to help you break up the sentences.

Practice introducing yourself and learn some useful replies on your CD.

3

What are they saying?

Write the correct number in the word balloons.

1 こんにちは。安紀子です。
konnichiwa. akiko desu.

2 実さん、こんにちは。
minoru san, konnichiwa.

3 さようなら。
sayounara.

4 優子さん、こんにちは。
yuuko san, konnichiwa.

What do you hear?

Work out the phrases below. Then listen and check (✔)
the two phrases you hear on your audio CD.

4

1 優子さん、さようなら。　☐

4 安紀子さん、こんにちは。　☐

2 正です。　☐

5 こんにちは。　☐

3 実さん、さようなら。　☐

5

 **Key Words**

お名前は(何ですか)
onamae wa (nan desu ka)? *what's your name?*

どうぞ
douzo *please*

ありがとうございます
arigatou gozaimasu *thank you*

おはようございます
ohayou gozaimasu *good morning*

こんばんは
konban wa *good evening*

 Language Focus

The full version of the question *What's your name?* お名前は何ですか。
onamae wa nan desu ka? is formed by combining お名前 **onamae** *(name)*
with the question word 何 **nan/nani** *(what?)*, です **desu** *(is)* and the question
marker か **ka**. は **wa** is a topic marker and can be roughly translated as *as for*.
Literally the question means "*as for name what is it?*"

Notice that we can shorten the question to: お名前は？ **onamae wa?** In this
case there is no question marker, so it is important to raise your voice at the
end of the question. This is less formal than the full version.

However, you should be aware that in Japan it is not so common to ask
someone's name directly. When meeting someone for the first time you would
usually introduce yourself, giving your family name first followed by your first
name. The other person would then do the same.

To introduce yourself, simply say *(name)* です **desu**. You can also add the
Japanese word for *I/me* (私 **watashi**) and the topic marker in front:
私は **watashi wa** *(name)* です **desu**.

Speaking practice

Practice the Japanese you have learned so far.

6

What does it mean?

Match the English word balloons to the Japanese.

For example: **1a**

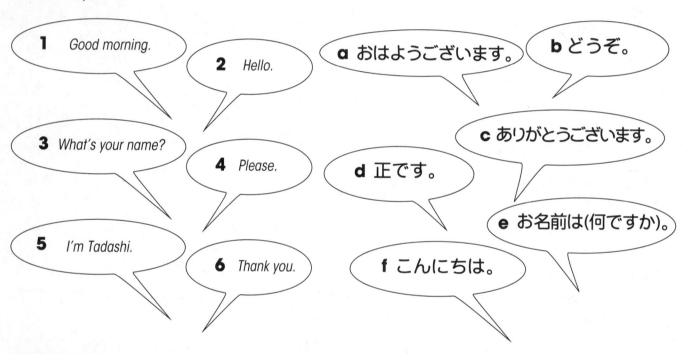

1 Good morning.

2 Hello.

a おはようございます。

b どうぞ。

3 What's your name?

4 Please.

c ありがとうございます。

d 正です。

5 I'm Tadashi.

6 Thank you.

e お名前は(何ですか)。

f こんにちは。

Which word?

Write the correct number of the word in the box
to complete the conversation, as in the example.

1正　2ございます
3は　4です
5おはよう

おはよう ___2___ 。
_____ ございます。
安紀子 _____ 。お名前 _____ ?
_____ です。

🔍 *Language Focus*

All of the words you have met so far have been written in either *hiragana* or *kanji* (Chinese characters).

The third writing system is *katakana*. This alphabet, or to be more accurate "syllabary," is used for all borrowed words including foreign names. As a general rule, katakana is squarer and less ornate than hiragana. You'll find a chart for katakana on page 91.

English names will be written in katakana but may be spelled slightly differently. Sarah for example is spelled セーラ **seera**. The ー that you see is used to make the previous vowel long, changing セ **se** to セー **see**. Names that include the English letter *l* are written with the letter *r*. So Helen becomes ヘレン **heren**.

What are their names?

Can you work out these common English names in Japanese script?
Use the katakana table on page 91 to help you work them out.

セーラ	*seera* Sarah	ピーター	_____
ヘレン	_____	ケン	_____
メリー	_____	マーク	_____
リサ	_____	ロバート	_____
ハナ	_____	ジェームス	_____

In or out?

Who is in the office today and who is out at meetings? Look at the wallchart and write the names in English in the correct column, as in the example.

セーラ	✔
実	✔
ジェームス	✘
優子	✔
ロバート	✘
安紀子	✘
ケン	✔
正	✔
ヘレン	✘
メリー	✘

IN	OUT
Sarah	

The Name Game

① Tear out Game Card 1 at the back of your book and cut out the name cards (leave the sentence-build cards at the bottom of the sheet for the moment).

② Put the cards Japanese side up and see if you can recognize the names. Turn over the cards to see if you were correct.

③ Keep shuffling the cards and testing yourself until you can read all the names.

④ Then cut out the extra sentence-build cards at the bottom of the sheet and make mini-dialogs. For example:

GAME CARD ❶ (see page 13)

Name cards:

安紀子	優子	正	実
セーラ	ヘレン	メリー	リサ
ロバート	ピーター	ケン	マーク

Sentence-build cards:

	こんにちは	さようなら	です
さん	何	お名前	か
?	は	ありがとうございます	
。	こんばんは	おはようございます	

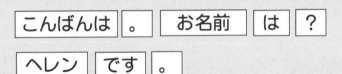

こんばんは	。	お名前	は	?

ヘレン	です	。

– **konban wa. onamae wa?**

– **heren desu.**

正　Tadashi

セーラ　Sarah

⑤ You can also play with a friend. Make mini-dialogs for each other to read. If you both have a book, you can play Pairs (pelmanism) with both sets of sentence-build cards, saying the words as you turn over the cards.

Key Words

日本 nihon/nippon	*Japan*	
中国 chuugoku	*China*	
韓国 kankoku	*Korea*	
アメリカ amerika	*America*	
イギリス igirisu	*England*	
カナダ kanada	*Canada*	
アイルランド airurando	*Ireland*	
オーストラリア oosutoraria	*Australia*	
国 kuni	*country*	
市 shi	*city*	

Notice how Japan and other countries in the region are written in kanji, but Western country names, such as America, are written phonetically in katakana.

To learn new words, try covering the English and looking at the Japanese script and pronunciation. Start from the first word and work your way to the last word seeing if you can remember the English. Then do the same but this time starting from the bottom and moving up to the first word. See if you can go down and up three times without making any mistakes. Then try looking only at the Japanese characters and see if you can remember the pronunciation and meaning. When you can recognize all the words, cover the Japanese and this time look at the English saying the Japanese out loud.

Where are the countries?

Write the number next to the country, as in the example.

カナダ _1_	イギリス ___	日本 ___	オーストラリア ___
韓国 ___	アイルランド ___	アメリカ ___	中国 ___

How do you say it?

Join the English to the pronunciation and the Japanese script, as in the example.

England	kuni	中国
Korea	igirisu	オーストラリア
Ireland	kanada	国
city	kankoku	アイルランド
China	shi	市
Canada	airurando	イギリス
America	oosutoraria	韓国
country	nihon/nippon	アメリカ
Australia	chuugoku	日本
Japan	amerika	カナダ

Where are the cities?

Now look at these cities and make sentences like this, using the phrase **にあります**
ni arimasu, for example:

東京は日本にあります。　**toukyou wa nihon ni arimasu.**　*Tokyo is in Japan.*

Tokyo	*New York*	*Washington*	*Los Angeles*
東京	ニューヨーク	ワシントン	ロサンジェルス
toukyou	**nyuuyooku**	**washinton**	**rosanjerusu**
Osaka	*Sydney*	*London*	*Dublin*
大阪	シドニー	ロンドン	ダブリン
oosaka	**shidonii**	**rondon**	**daburin**

Language Focus

When talking about where we come from in Japanese it is more common to refer to our nationality. This is very simple to do. Simply add the word for person, 人 **jin**, to the country, followed by です **desu** (*I am*).

> アメリカ人です。 **amerikajin desu.** *I'm American.*
>
> 日本人です。 **nihonjin desu.** *I'm Japanese.*

If you wish to specify the town or city you come from you would use the formula *town/city* + から来ました **kara kimashita**. から **kara** means *from* and 来ました **kimashita** means *have come*. You can say what town/city and what country you come from in the same sentence linking them with の **no** (*"of"*):

> イギリスのロンドンから来ました。
> **igirisu no rondon kara kimashita.**
> *I'm from London in England.*

To ask the question ***What nationality are you?*** the word order is:
何 **nan/nani** *(what)* + 人 **jin** *(person)* + です **desu** + か **ka** *(question marker)*

> 何人ですか。 **nani jin desu ka?** *What nationality are you?*
>
> イギリス人です。 **igirisujin desu.** *I'm English.*

You can use どこ **doko** *(where?)* to ask someone what town/city they are from:

> どこから来ましたか。 **doko kara kimashita ka?**
> *Where are you from?*
>
> 大阪から来ました。 **oosaka kara kimashita.**
> *I'm from Osaka.*

 8 Listen to four different people introducing themselves and see if you can understand where they are from.

Where are they from?

Join the people to their nationalities, as in the example. Listen again to track 8 on your CD and look back at the names and countries if you need to remind yourself.

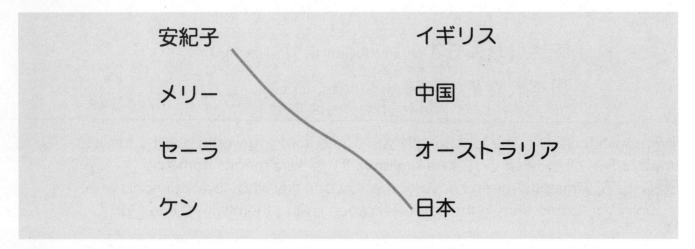

安紀子	イギリス
メリー	中国
セーラ	オーストラリア
ケン	日本

Where are you from?

Now say where you're from.
Follow the prompts on your audio CD.

9

 ## Key Words

10

人	jin/hito	*person*	から	kara	*from*
何	nan/nani	*what*	どこ	doko?	*where?*
さん	san	*Mr./Mrs./Ms./Miss*	か	ka?	*question marker*

 ## *Language Focus*

English refers to other people as he or she: *He is American*, *She is from New York*, etc. Japanese speakers rarely use the pronouns for *he, she, you*, etc. Instead they prefer to use the person's name followed by the title さん **san**.

> 安紀子さんは日本人です。
> **akiko san wa nihonjin desu.** *She (Akiko) is Japanese.*
>
> ケンさんは中国のペキンから来ました。
> **ken san wa chuugoku no pekin kara kimashita.**
> *He (Ken) is from Beijing in China.*

The question 何人ですか。 **nani jin desu ka?** can mean *What nationality are you/he/she/they?* etc. depending on who you are talking to, or about. To make it more specific you would need to use the person's name. Again さん **san** is needed after the name, together with the topic marker は **wa** ("*as for*").

> セーラさんは何人ですか。
> **seera san wa nani jin desu ka?**
> *Sarah, what nationality are you? (when talking <u>to</u> Sarah)* OR
> *What nationality is Sarah? (when talking <u>about</u> Sarah)*

This makes life very easy, but it does mean that you have to remember everyone's name!

You have probably noticed that the Japanese script doesn't use question marks very much. This is because the question marker か **ka** will indicate that the phrase is a question without the need to use an additional question mark. However if か **ka** is not used, such as in お名前は？ **onamae wa?** then you will usually see a question mark.

Who's from where?

Make questions and answers about where these people are from, as in the example.

1

ピーターさんは何人ですか。
piitaa san wa nani jin desu ka?
What nationality is Peter?

ピーターさんはアメリカ人です。
piitaa san wa amerikajin desu.
Peter is American.

2

安紀子

3

リサ

4

マーク

5

ジェームス

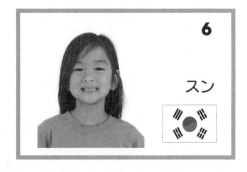

6

スン

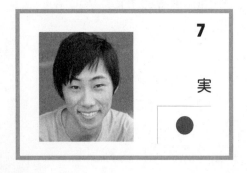

7

実

8

メリー

Listen and check

Listen to the conversation on your audio CD and decide if these sentences are true or false.

		True	False
1	The woman's name is Sophie.	☐	☐
2	She comes from Canada.	☐	☐
3	The man's name is Tadashi.	☐	☐
4	He comes from Japan.	☐	☐
5	They are already friends.	☐	☐

What does it mean?

Now read the Japanese you heard in the conversation and match it with the English, as in the example.

I'm from Canada.	はじめまして。 **hajimemashite**
He's from Japan.	カナダ人です。
My name's Lucy.	お名前は？
What's your name?	日本人です。
How do you do?	どうぞよろしく。 **douzo yoroshiku**
Pleased to meet you.	ルーシーです。

I'm from Canada is matched with カナダ人です。

What does it mean?

Try to work out each of these sentences. It will help if you break them up into the separate words and phrases. Look back at the Key Word panels if you need help.

Then read the sentences out loud when you have figured them out and write the English next to each, as in the example.

1 ルーシーです。　　　　　　　　　　*I'm Lucy*

2 カナダ人です。

3 優子さんは日本人です。

4 お名前は？

5 安紀子です。

6 ピーターさんは何人ですか。

7 ジェームスさんはイギリス人です。

8 アメリカ人です。

You can compare your pronunciation of the sentences with the models on your audio CD.

12

Now complete this description of yourself. Read the sentences out loud, adding your own details.

…です。

…の… から来ました。

The Flag Game

1. Tear out Game Card 2.

2. Find a die and counter(s).

3. Put the counter(s) on START.

4. Throw the die and move that number of squares.

5. When you land on a flag, you must ask and answer the appropriate question for that country. For example:

何人ですか。   nani jin desu ka?
What nationality are you?

イギリス人です。 igirisujin desu.
I'm English.

6. If you can't remember the question or answer, you must go back to the square you came from. You must throw the exact number to finish.

7. You can challenge yourself or play with a friend.

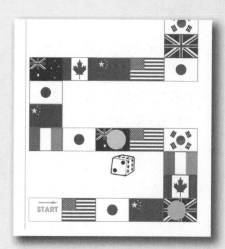

Key Words

13

椅子 **isu**	chair		ドア **doa**	door
テーブル **teeberu**	table		窓 **mado**	window
テレビ **terebi**	television		ペン **pen**	pen
本 **hon**	book		雑誌 **zasshi**	magazine
かばん **kaban**	bag		ソファー **sofaa**	sofa
コンピュータ **konpyuuta**	computer		電話 **denwa**	telephone

Notice how all three writing systems are represented in the words above.

Original Japanese words are written in either kanji, for example 本 **hon** (*book*) and 窓 **mado** (*window*), or in hiragana, for example かばん **kaban** (*bag*).

Loan words are written in katakana, for example ソファー **sofaa** (*sofa*) and テレビ **terebi** (*television*).

Language Focus

Japanese nouns do not have articles (*a/an, the*). Plurals are also very simple – there aren't any! So 本 **hon** can mean *book*, *a book*, *the book*, *books*, or *the books*.

What does it mean?

Match the Japanese with the pictures, then write the pronunciation and the English, as in the example.

Japanese	Pronunciation & English
ソファー	_____
電話	_____
ドア	_____
窓	*mado window(s)*
ペン	_____
かばん	_____
コンピュータ	_____
椅子	_____
テーブル	_____
テレビ	_____
本	_____
雑誌	_____

Word Square

Can you find the 8 key words in the word square? Circle them and write the English, as in the example. The words can be horizontal or vertical.

小	園	ラ	ソ	テ	ー	ブ	ル
か	ば	ん	ス	レ	髪	港	ン
さ	公	で	さ	ビ	園	車	本
お	電	空	よ	タ	フ	ク	す
こ	コ	ン	ピ	ュ	ー	タ	あ
レ	ー	毛	い	腹	テ	ら	そ
ト	雑	誌	う	の	な	椅	こ
ソ	フ	ァ	ー	公	シ	子	シ

computer

_____

_____

_____

_____

_____

_____

_____

Odd One Out

Which is the odd one out? Circle the word that doesn't belong in each row.

椅子 * テーブル * お名前 * ソファー

電話 * 日本 * アメリカ * 韓国

安紀子 * ペン * ロバート * セーラ

かばん * こんばんは * さようなら * こんにちは

何 * か * どこ * ドア

Language Focus

We have already met the words for *what*, 何 nan/nani, and *is*, です desu.
Using these we can ask *What is it?/What are they?*:

> 何ですか。 **nan desu ka?**   *What is it?/What are they?*
>
> 椅子です。 **isu desu.** *It's a chair./They're chairs.*

To ask *What's this?/What's that?* Japanese makes a distinction depending on
the position of the object being talked about:

これ **kore** *this thing here:* when the object is near to the speaker

それ **sore** *that thing there:* when the object is nearer to the listener

あれ **are** *that thing over there:* when the object is far away from both
listener and speaker

A question asked with これ **kore** would therefore usually be answered using それ **sore**
and vice versa. Questions asked with あれ **are** are usually answered also using あれ **are**.

> これは何ですか。
> **kore wa nan desu ka?**
> *What's this (thing here)?*
> ⟶
> それはテーブルです。
> **sore wa teeberu desu.**
> *That (thing there) is a table.*
>
> あれは何ですか。
> **are wa nan desu ka?**
> *What's that (thing over there)?*
> ⟶
> あれはかばんです。
> **are wa kaban desu.**
> *That (thing over there) is a bag.*

A *yes/no* question can be answered using either いいえ iie (*no*) or the useful phrase
はい、そうです hai, sou desu (*yes, that's right*).

> それは本ですか。   **sore wa hon desu ka.** *Is that a book?*
>
> いいえ、これは雑誌です。   はい、そうです。
> **iie, kore wa zasshi desu.**   **hai, sou desu.**
> *No, this is a magazine.*   *Yes, that's right.*

Your turn to speak

Now ask what things are. Follow the prompts on your audio CD.

14

What is it?

Look at the photos of everyday objects from unusual angles. Then read the sentences and decide which picture they describe, as in the example.

1 椅子です。 _e_   **5** ドアです。 _____

2 コンピュータです。 _____   **6** テレビです。 _____

3 ソファーです。 _____   **7** ペンです。 _____

4 電話です。 _____   **8** かばんです。 _____

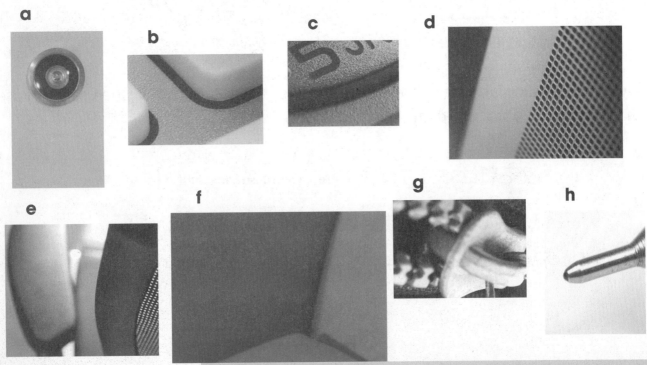

a b c d

e f g h

 **Key Words**

15

紅茶	koocha	*black tea*	サンドイッチ sandoicchi	*sandwich*
お茶	ocha	*green tea*	そば soba	*noodles*
コーヒー	koohii	*coffee*	豚カツ tonkatsu	*pork cutlet*
ケーキ	keeki	*cake*		

 Language Focus

To request an item in Japanese we use the following pattern:
item + をお願いします **o onegaishimasu**:

コーヒーをお願いします。 **koohii o onegaishimasu.** *I'd like a coffee.*

To request more than one item simply link them using と **to** (*and*):

コーヒーとサンドイッチをお願いします。
koohii to sandoicchi o onegaishimasu.
I'd like a coffee and a sandwich.

Having asked for an item you will hear the word どうぞ **douzo** (*please*) when it is handed to you.

お茶をどうぞ。
ocha o douzo.
Here's your green tea. ("green tea, please")

ありがとうございます。
arigatou gozaimasu.
Thank you.

Who orders what?

16

What are the customers ordering? Listen to your CD and check what they order, as in the example.

Note that when you enter a shop or restaurant, etc., you will be welcomed with a shout of いらっしゃいませ irasshaimase (*can I help you?*), rather than *hello*.

	black tea	green tea	coffee	sandwich	cake	noodles	pork cutlet
Customer 1			✓		✓		
Customer 2							
Customer 3							
Customer 4							
Customer 5							

Now look at the table above and pretend you are ordering for yourself.

コーヒーとケーキをお願いします。 koohii to keeki o onegaishimasu.

Unscramble the conversation

Can you put this conversation in the correct order?
(Note that じゃあ jaa means *well, then*.)

a コーヒーをお願いします。
koohii o onegaishimasu.

b ありがとうございます。
arigatou gozaimasu.

c これは何ですか。
kore wa nan desu ka?

d コーヒーと豚カツをどうぞ。
koohii to tonkatsu o douzo.

f 豚カツです。
tonkatsu desu.

e はい、コーヒーですね。
hai, koohii desu ne.

g いらっしゃいませ。
irasshaimase.

h じゃあ、豚カツをお願いします。
jaa, tonkatsu o onegaishimasu.

ORDER: *g,* _____

Now check your answer with the conversation on your audio CD.

17

At the café

Your turn to order now. Look at the menu below and then you'll be
ready to order from the waiter on your CD.

紅茶

お茶

コーヒー

サンドイッチ

ケーキ

そば

豚カツ

The Café Game

1. Cut out the picture cards from Game Card 3.

2. Put the cards into a bag.

3. Shake the bag.

4. Pull out a card without looking.

5. Ask for the item on the card. For example:

お茶をお願いします。

ocha o onegaishimasu.

I'd like a green tea.

6. If you can ask the question out loud quickly and fluently, then put the card aside. If not, then put it back into the bag.

7. See how long it takes you to get all of the cards out of the bag. Or play with a friend and see who can collect the most cards.

 *Key Words*

部屋	heya	room	家	ie	house
冷蔵庫	reizouko	refrigerator	木	ki	trees
戸棚	todana	cupboard	車	kuruma	car
レンジ	renji	stove	猫	neko	cat
ベッド	beddo	bed	犬	inu	dog
絵	e	picture	ネズミ	nezumi	mouse

19

Japanese kanji words can be a single character, such as 犬 inu (*dog*) or 車 kuruma (*car*), or a combination of two or more characters, such as 部屋 heya (*room*) or 冷蔵庫 reizouko (*refrigerator*).

Sometimes you can find common characters, such as 茶 cha (*tea*), which you have met in 紅茶 koocha (*black tea*) and お茶 ocha (*green tea*).

Looking out for common characters can help you remember kanji.

A word of warning: sometimes the same kanji character is pronounced differently in combination. For example, 国 kuni (*country*) but 中国 chuugoku (*China*).

What does it mean?

Join the Japanese to the pronunciation and write down the meaning in English.

絵	nezumi	_____
部屋	renji	_____
冷蔵庫	ki	_____
木	kuruma	_____
ネズミ	e	*picture*
ベッド	neko	_____
車	todana	_____
猫	ie	_____
戸棚	inu	_____
犬	beddo	_____
レンジ	heya	_____
家	reizouko	_____

What can you see?

Look at the picture and check (✔) the things you can see, as in the example.

レンジ	☐	ベッド	☑
冷蔵庫	☐	戸棚	☐
絵	☐	木	☐
コンピュータ	☐	猫	☐
テーブル	☐	椅子	☐
車	☐	本	☐
窓	☐	犬	☐
ペン	☐	かばん	☐
雑誌	☐	ネズミ	☐

Key Words

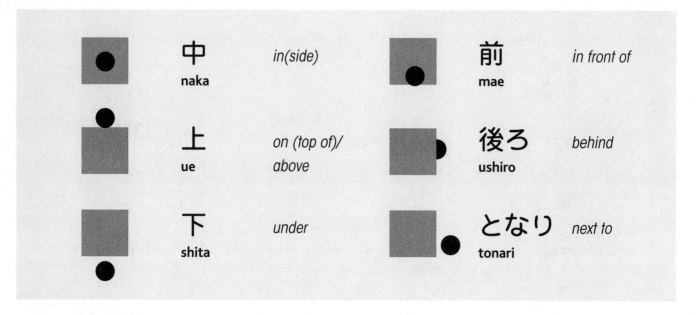

中 **naka**	in(side)	
上 **ue**	on (top of)/ above	
下 **shita**	under	
前 **mae**	in front of	
後ろ **ushiro**	behind	
となり **tonari**	next to	

Language Focus

To say where something is in English we simply place the preposition (positional word) in the middle of the two objects: ***The book is <u>on</u> the table***. In Japanese the preposition comes at the end of the sentence:

> 本はテーブルの上です。
>
> **hon wa teeburu no ue desu.**   *The book is on the table.*

As in English the object whose location we are describing comes at the start of the sentence, and is marked by the topic marker は **wa** (*"as for"*). Notice that the particle の **no** is needed after the second item and before the preposition. The sentence finishes with です **desu** (*is*). We are literally saying: "***book as for table on top of is***."

Practice saying where things are on your CD.

21

Which word?

Put a circle around the word that correctly
describes each picture, as in the example.

車は家の （前） です。
　　　　　後ろ

ベッドは窓の 上 です。
　　　　　　下

絵はソファーの 前 です。
　　　　　　　上

コンピュータはテーブルの 上 です。
　　　　　　　　　　　となり

冷蔵庫はレンジの となり です。
　　　　　　　　上

猫は椅子の 後ろ です。
　　　　　　下

犬は車の 中 です。
　　　　　下

Language Focus

…があります **ga arimasu** or …がいます **ga imasu** are useful when we wish to express simple descriptive phrases, the equivalent of the English *there is/there are*.

がいます **ga imasu** is used when we are talking about *animate* items (e.g., people or animals). があります **ga arimasu** is used to talk about *inanimate* items (e.g., objects such as books):

> 犬がいます。 **inu ga imasu.**
> *There is a dog./There are some dogs.*
>
> 本があります。 **hon ga arimasu.**
> *There is a book./There are some books.*

To form the question *is there/are there?* simply add か **ka?** on the end:

> 本がありますか。 **hon ga arimasu ka?**
> *Is there a book?/Are there any books?*

We can now combine this model with the prepositions we have already met to produce fuller descriptions. Notice the word order and the additional particle に **ni** before the second half of the sentence:

> テーブルの上に本があります。
> **teeburu no ue ni hon ga arimasu.**
> *There is a book on the table. (table on top of – book there is)*
>
> 木の前に犬がいます。
> **ki no mae ni inu ga imasu.**
> *There is a dog in front of the tree. (tree in front of – dog there is)*

> Look around the room you are in at the moment, or think of a room you know well. Can you describe where some of the things are, using があります **ga arimasu** or がいます **ga imasu**?

Where are the mice?

See how many mice you can find in the picture and make sentences about them using the sentence table, as in the example.

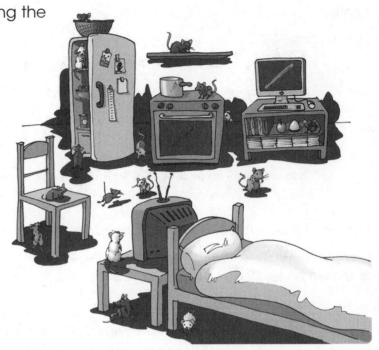

Example:

レンジの上にネズミがいます。

renji no ue ni nezumi ga imasu.

There's a mouse on top of the stove.

テーブル teeburu			
椅子 isu			
冷蔵庫 reizouko		中 naka	
ソファー sofaa		上 ue	
戸棚 todana	の no	下 shita	にネズミがいます。
レンジ renji		後ろ ushiro	ni nezumi ga imasu.
テレビ terebi		前 mae	
コンピュータ konpyuuta		となり tonari	
ベッド beddo			

Language Focus

We have been using the word です desu, meaning *is/am/are*, in many of the sentences we have learned so far:

日本人です。 nihonjin desu. *I'm Japanese.*

セーラさんはイギリス人です。
seera san wa igirisujin desu. *Sarah is English.*

本はテレビの上です。
hon wa terebi no ue desu. *The book is on top of the television.*

But what if we wish to express a negative? To turn a positive です desu statement into a negative one simply change です desu to ではありません de wa arimasen or じゃありません ja arimasen:

日本人ではありません/じゃありません。
nihonjin de wa arimasen/ja arimasen. *I'm not Japanese.*

本はテレビの上ではありません/じゃありません。
hon wa terebi no ue de wa arimasen/ja arimasen. *The book is not on top of the television.*

To make a があります ga arimasu/がいます ga imasu sentence negative change が ga to は wa and ます masu to ません masen:

テーブルの上に雑誌はありません。
teeburu no ue ni zasshi wa arimasen. *There isn't a magazine on the table.*

ソファーの後ろにネズミはいません。
sofaa no ushiro ni nezumi wa imasen. *There isn't a mouse behind the sofa.*

No it isn't!

Practice disagreeing! Go to your audio CD and contradict all the statements you hear.

22

True or False?

Decide if the sentences describing the picture are true or false, as in the example.

	True	False
部屋には冷蔵庫があります。	☑	☐
部屋にはベッドがあります。	☐	☐
電話はテーブルの上です。	☐	☐
戸棚があります。	☐	☐
窓があります。	☐	☐
テーブルの下にネズミはいません。	☐	☐
家の後ろに木があります。	☐	☐
レンジは冷蔵庫のとなりです。	☐	☐
テーブルの下に犬がいます。	☐	☐
部屋にはテレビはありません。	☐	☐

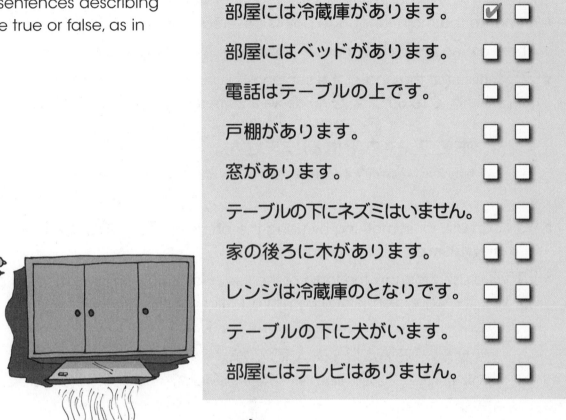

Language Review

You're half way through this program – congratulations! This is a good time to summarize the main language points covered so far in *Read & Speak Japanese*.

1 There are no plural differences in Japanese: 木 ki means both *tree* and *trees.*

2 です desu (at the end of the sentence) is used to express *am/is/are.* The opposite is ではありません de wa arimasen or じゃありません ja arimasen.

> 本です。/本ではありません。
> **hon desu. / hon de wa arimasen.** *It's a book./It isn't a book.*

3 You can ask for something by using the phrase ...をお願いします
...o onegaishimasu (*I'd like a/some...*).

4 は wa is used to mark the topic of the sentence and can be translated as *as for.* か ka is the equivalent of the English question mark.

> 安紀子さんは日本人ですか。
> **akiko san wa nihonjin desu ka?** *Is Akiko Japanese? ("as for akiko, she is Japanese ka?")*

5 Different words are used for *this/that* depending on the location of the object being talked about: これ kore (*object near speaker*); それ sore (*object near listener*); and あれ are (*object far from speaker <u>and</u> listener*).

6 Prepositions (*in/on/under, etc.*) in Japanese are placed in different positions in the sentence than in English. *There is/there are* is があります ga arimasu for inanimate objects and がいます ga imasu for animate beings. The opposites are はありません wa arimasen and はいません wa imasen. Notice these Japanese structures in comparison with the English:

> 電話は椅子の上です。
> **denwa wa isu no ue desu.** *The telephone is on the chair.*
>
> ケーキはありません。
> **keeki wa arimasen.** *There isn't any cake.*
>
> テーブルの下に犬がいます。
> **teeburu no shita ni inu ga imasu.** *There's a dog under the table.*

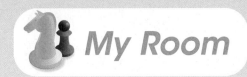

My Room

1. Tear out Game Card 4 at the back of your book and cut out the small pictures of items around the house (leave the sentence-build cards at the bottom of the sheet for the moment).

2. Stick the pictures wherever you like on the scene below.

3. Cut out the sentence-build cards from Game Card 4. Make as many sentences as you can describing your room. For example:

| 窓 | の | となり | に | 絵 | があります | 。 |

mado no tonari ni e ga arimasu.

Sentence-build cards:

中	上	下	
後ろ	となり	がいます	がぁ
はいません	はありません	です	
。	ベッド	テーブル	ソ
窓	椅子	テレビ	コンヒ
電話	絵	ネズミ	ネ
猫	サンドイッチ	の	に

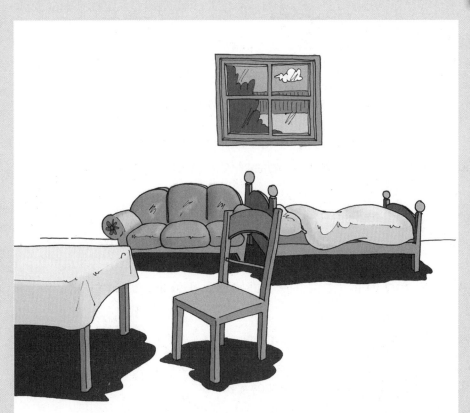

Key Words

23

大きい	ookii	big	長い	nagai	long
小さい	chiisai	small	短い	mijikai	short
古い	furui	old	高い	takai	expensive
新しい	atarashii	new	安い	yasui	inexpensive
			とても	totemo	very

Language Focus

Adjectives in Japanese are very easy to use. As in English they can come either before the noun they describe:

大きい犬
ookii inu *(a) big dog*

高い車
takai kuruma *(an) expensive car*

Or, in a sentence with **desu** (*am/is/are*), after the noun they describe.
Notice the word order: *item* + **wa** (*"as for"*) + *adjective* + **desu** (*is*):

犬は大きいです。
inu wa ookii desu. *The dog is big.*

車は高いです。
kuruma wa takai desu. *The car is expensive.*

とても **totemo** (*very*) is placed in front of the adjective, just like in English:

とても大きい犬
totemo ookii inu *(a) very big dog*

犬はとても大きいです。
inu wa totemo ookii desu.
The dog is very big.

44

Can you remember?

Cover the Key Words panel on page 44. Then see if you can write out the pronunciation and meaning of the words below, as in the example.

安い	y a s u i	*inexpensive*
古い	f _ _ i	_____
とても	t _ _ _ m _	_____
短い	_ i _ _ a _	_____
小さい	_ h _ _ s _ _	_____
長い	n _ _ _ _	_____
大きい	_ _ _ _ i	_____
新しい	a _ a _ _ s _ _ _	_____
高い	t _ _ _ i	_____

All the adjectives above are written in a combination of kanji characters and a hiragana ending. This is reasonably common in Japanese, and you will meet more examples as you progress.

What does it mean?

Match the Japanese with the pictures. Then read the Japanese out loud and write the English next to each, as in the example.

新しいソファー _____

小さいコーヒー _____

小さい犬 *(a) small dog* _____

とても古い車 _____

小さいネズミ _____

大きいサンドイッチ _____

安い絵 _____

大きい木 _____

Listen and check

Listen to the conversation at the car rental company and decide if these sentences are true or false. (Note that ちょっと **chotto** means *a little* and どうですか **dou desu ka** means *how about?*)

		True	False
1	The conversation takes place in the evening	☐	☐
2	The woman wants to rent a car.	☐	☐
3	She thinks the first car is very expensive.	☐	☐
4	She thinks the second car is too big.	☐	☐
5	She likes the third car.	☐	☐

Unscramble the sentences

Look at the scrambled sentences below and write the correct order.

Example ("Good morning"): ⓑ ございます ⓐ おはよう

1 ☐ です ☐ アメリカ ☐ 人

2 ☐ ちょっと ☐ は ☐ です ☐ 高い ☐ 車

3 ☐ 小さい ☐ です ☐ 車 ☐ は

4 ☐ は ☐ ですか ☐ どう ☐ これ

Language Focus

English uses the verb *to have* when talking about i) personal possession (*I have a car*) and ii) availability of items (*Do you have any sandwiches?* i.e. *Are there any sandwiches?*). Japanese makes a distinction between these two uses.

When you use the English *have* to mean *possess* the Japanese equivalent is を持っています o motteimasu:

> 私は古いコンピュータを持っています。
> **watashi wa furui konpyuuta o motteimasu.** *I have an old computer.*

To say what someone else owns, use the person's name followed by さん san:

> ピーターさんは新しい車を持っています。
> **piiitaa san wa atarashii kuruma o motteimasu.** *Peter has a new car.*

To ask someone if they own a particular item say:

name さん、*item* を持っていますか。

> ヘレンさん、車を持っていますか。
> **heren san, kuruma o motteimasu ka.** *Helen, do you have a car?*

When using *have* to express availability, Japanese uses the verbs あります arimasu and います imasu – which we have met for talking about existence (see page 38). This is useful when enquiring about the availability of goods.

Now you can take part in a conversation with the car rental company. Follow the prompts on your audio CD.

25

You will need one new phrase:
ちょうどいいですね。
choudo ii desu ne. (*That's perfect.*)

26

 *Key Words*

足 ashi	*leg*		髪の毛 kami no ke*	*hair*	
腕 ude	*arm*		頭 atama	*head*	
指 yubi	*fingers*		鼻 hana	*nose*	
目 me	*eyes*		口 kuchi	*mouth*	
耳 mimi	*ears*		お腹 onaka	*stomach*	

*髪の毛 kami no ke is used to refer to human hair (on the head).
毛 ke alone means any hair, including animal hair.

By now you're probably feeling much more confident about reading and speaking Japanese. Maybe you'd like to try writing the letters and characters for yourself. Although it's fun to copy the simpler shapes, you will need to get a guide to writing Japanese in order to form them correctly. The strokes should be completed in a certain order and the kanji particularly will need plenty of practice to perfect.

Which word?

Circle the correct word to match the translation, as in the example.

1	head	家	頭	椅子	本
2	leg	目	窓	鼻	足
3	stomach	車	日本	お腹	髪の毛
4	mouth	鼻	雑誌	口	猫
5	fingers	指	足	目	かばん
6	hair	木	足	国	髪の毛
7	ears	頭	ドア	市	耳
8	nose	指	鼻	ペン	市
9	eyes	鼻	電話	目	中国
10	arm	腕	犬	頭	指

首 = kubi

尾 = tail

At the pet show

Can you use the words in the box to complete the description of these pets?

1 鼻	**2** です	**3** 耳
4 は	**5** 大きい	**6** 長い

この猫は毛が __6__ です。足も長い ____ 。____ が小さいです。

この犬 ____ 毛が短いです。____ がとても小さいです。
口が ____ です。

What does he look like?

What does the creature look like? Make as many sentences
as you can describing what it looks like.

We've included some extra parts of the body you could use in your description.

Example:

尾がとても長いです。

o ga totemo nagai desu.

(His) tail is very long.

翼 **tsubasa** *wings*

首 **kubi** *neck*

尾 **o** *tail*

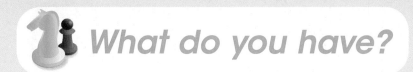

What do you have?

1. Cut out the picture cards from Game Card 5 and put them in a bag.

2. Cut out the adjective cards and put them in a different bag.

3. Pull out one card from each bag without looking.

4. Make a sentence to match the cards you have chosen, for example:

   私は古いコンピュータを持っています。

   watashi wa furui konpyuuta o motteimasu.

   I have an old computer.

5. Keep playing until all the cards have been chosen.

6. You can put the cards back in the bag and start again – each time the sentences will be different.

 *Key Words*

空港 **kuukou**	*airport*	公園 **kouen**	*park*
学校 **gakkou**	*school*	橋 **hashi**	*bridge*
ホテル **hoteru**	*hotel*	…道り …**douri**	*… Street*
銀行 **ginkou**	*bank*	なかみせ通り **nakamise douri**	Nakamise Street
レストラン **resutoran**	*restaurant*	…はどこですか。 **…wa doko desu ka?**	*where is/are…?*
駅 **eki**	*station*	あそこ **asoko**	*over there*

28 You are new in town and are asking a Japanese friend about the facilities. Follow the prompts on your audio CD.

Language Focus

Notice the words for *hotel* and *restaurant*. They are examples of 外来語 gairaigo words borrowed from other languages. Japanese has borrowed many words from other languages, particularly English. Look back at Topic 3. The words for *sandwich*, *cake*, and *coffee* are all examples of **gairaigo**.

You can recognize these words although they will sound slightly different and often longer since they are adapted to Japanese pronunciation. **Gairaigo** words are always written in katakana script.

Questions and answers

Match the questions with their answers, as in the example.

銀行はどこですか。 — 橋はあそこです。

レストランはありますか。 はい、レストランがあります。

ホテルはありますか。 公園は学校のとなりです。

公園はどこですか。 銀行は学校のとなりです。

橋はどこですか。 駅の前にホテルがあります。

 ## Key Words

タクシー **takushii**	*taxi*	船 **fune**	*boat*
バス **basu**	*bus*	自転車 **jitensha**	*bicycle*
電車 **densha**	*train*	飛行機 **hikouki**	*plane*

Language Focus

The particle で **de** can be used after a mode of transportation to mean *by*.

車で **kuruma de** *by car*

タクシーで **takushii de** *by taxi*

バスで **basu de** *by bus*

船で **fune de** *by boat*

Word Square

Can you find the seven different means of transportation in the word square?
Write out the pronunciation and meaning for the words you have found,
as in the example.

駅	船	ラ	ソ	飛	行	機	ル
か	ば	ん	ス	レ	髪	港	ン
バ	公	で	さ	ビ	園	電	車
ー	タ	ク	シ	ー	フ	ク	す
こ	コ	ン	ピ	ュ	ー	タ	あ
レ	ー	毛	い	腹	テ	ら	そ
ト	バ	ス	う	の	な	車	こ
道	フ	ァ	自	転	車	子	シ

kuruma (car)

_____

_____

_____

_____

_____

_____

Key Words

すみません。			まっすぐ行って下さい	
sumimasen	.Excuse me.		massugu itte kudasai	*go straight ahead*
...はどうやって行きますか。			電車で行きます	
...wa dou yatte ikimasu ka?	*How do I get to...?*		densha de ikimasu	*go by train*
曲がる magaru	*to turn*		タクシーで行きます	
			takushii de ikimasu	*go by taxi*
...曲がって下さい				
...magatte kudasai	*please turn...*		それから sore kara	*then*
右 migi	*right*		博物館 hakubutsukan	*museum*
左 hidari	*left*		バス停 basutei	*bus stop*

Ask where places are around town. Follow the prompts on your audio CD.

31

Language Focus

To ask for directions use **...はどこですか** *...wa doko desu ka?* (*Where is/are...?*) or
...はどうやって行きますか *...wa dou yatte ikimasu ka?* (*How do I get to...?*):

銀行はどこですか。

ginkou wa doko desu ka? *Where is the bank?*

公園はどうやって行きますか。

kouen wa dou yatte ikimasu ka? *How do I get to the park?*

When replying, the direction **右 migi** (*right*) or **左 hidari** (*left*) comes first in the sentence, followed by the particle **ni** and then **曲がって下さい** **magatte kudasai** (*please turn*):

右に曲がって下さい。	左に曲がって下さい。
migi ni magatte kudasai.	**hidari ni magatte kudasai.**
(Please) turn right.	*(Please) turn left.*

Here are two possible dialogs:

–すみません、駅はどこですか。
sumimasen, eki wa doko desu ka? *Excuse me. Where's the station?*

–まっすぐ行って下さい。それから右に曲がって下さい。
駅はホテルのとなりです。 **massugu itte kudasai.**
sore kara migi ni magatte kudasai. eki wa hoteru no tonari desu.
Go straight ahead. Then turn right. The station is next to the hotel.

–すみません、空港はどうやって行きますか。
sumimasen, kuukou wa dou yatte ikimasu ka?
Excuse me. How do I get to the airport?

–バスで行きます。 **basu de ikimasu.** *Go by bus.*

Which way?

Make questions and answers, as in the example.

すみません、駅はどこですか。
sumimasen, eki wa doko desu ka?
Excuse me, where's the station?

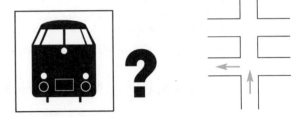

左に曲がって下さい。
hidari ni magatte kudasai.
Turn left.

1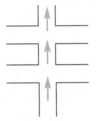

2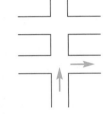

3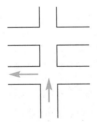

4

5

6

Around town

Below is a plan of a small town with some landmarks shown.
Starting from **You are here**, try to give directions to the following places:

駅	病院	公園	バス停
eki	**byouin**	**kouen**	**basutei**
the station	*the hospital*	*the park*	*the bus stop*

For example, your directions to the station could be something like this:

まっすぐ行って下さい。それから右に曲がって下さい。
駅は橋のとなりです。

massugu itte kudasai. sore kara migi ni magatte kudasai. eki wa hashi no tonari desu.

Go straight ahead. Then turn right. The station is next to the bridge.

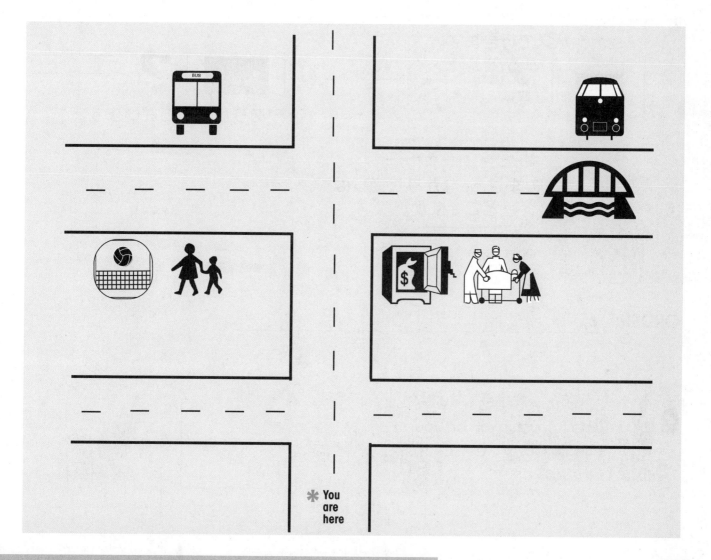

Unscramble the conversation

See if you can read the Japanese in the word balloons. Then put the conversation in the correct order.

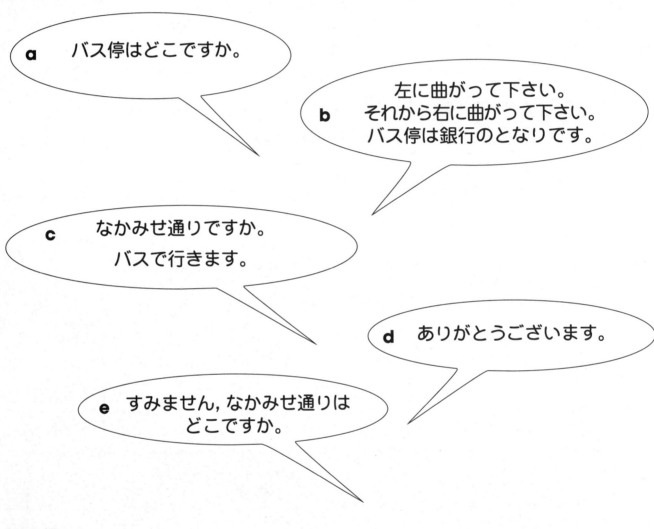

a バス停はどこですか。

b 左に曲がって下さい。
それから右に曲がって下さい。
バス停は銀行のとなりです。

c なかみせ通りですか。
バスで行きます。

d ありがとうございます。

e すみません, なかみせ通りは
どこですか。

ORDER: _e,_ _____

Check your answer with the conversation on your audio CD.

32

11/5/2018

TAKITA JENNIFER L

Item Number: 31901051227843

All Contra Costa County Libraries will be
closed on November 11th, 12th, and 22nd. In
addition, Prewett Library GenOn Gateway
Center for Learning will be closed Friday,
November 23rd, and all libraries will close by
6:00 p.m. on Wednesday, November 21st.
Items may be renewed at ccclib.org or by
calling 1-800-984-4636, menu option 1.
Book drops will be open. El Sobrante Library
remains closed for repairs.

Hold Shelf Slip

Town Planning

33

1. Cut out the pictures of places around town from Game Card 6.

2. Listen to the first set of directions for the bank on your audio CD.

3. Pause the CD and stick the picture of the bank in the correct place on the town map on your game card.

4. Listen to the next set of directions and stick down the appropriate picture.

5. Repeat for all the directions until you have all your pictures stuck down on the map. (Note that 裏 ura also means *behind* and 側 gawa means *side*.)

6. Looking at the completed map, you could try to give directions to the various places yourself. For example:

まっすぐ行って下さい。
それから左に曲がって下さい。
銀行は学校のとなりです。

massugu itte kudasai. sore kara hidari
ni magatte kudasai. ginkou wa gakkou
no tonari desu.

*(Go straight ahead. Then turn left.
The bank is next to the school.)*

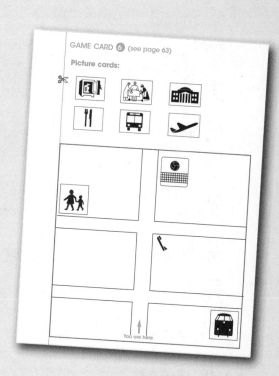

Key Words

34

妻	tsuma	*my wife*	奥さん	okusan	*wife*
夫	otto	*my husband*	ご主人	goshujin	*husband*
母	haha	*my mother*	お母さん	okaasan	*mother*
父	chichi	*my father*	お父さん	otousan	*father*
姉	ane	*my older sister*	お姉さん	oneesan	*older sister*
妹	imouto	*my younger sister*	妹さん	imoutosan	*younger sister*
兄	ani	*my older brother*	お兄さん	oniisan	*older brother*
弟	otouto	*my younger brother*	弟さん	otoutosan	*younger brother*
娘	musume	*my daughter*	お嬢さん	ojousan	*daughter*
息子	musuko	*my son*	息子さん	musukosan	*son*
			子供	kodomo	*children*

Japanese has two sets of words for family members, one meaning *my* mother, *my* older sister, etc., and one meaning someone else's mother, older sister, etc. The meaning of *my*, *your*, etc. is communicated within the word itself and there is no need for a separate word to express possession.

Note that the polite way to ask someone if they have children is お子さんがいますか **okosan ga imasu ka**. And the polite way to ask if someone has siblings is ご兄弟がいますか **gokyoudai ga imasu ka**.

Language Focus

You can make sentences to talk about your family using the verb がいます
ga imasu (*to exist:* for living objects) and its opposite はいません wa imasen,
which you have already met (see pages 38 and 40):

> 姉がいます。 **ane ga imasu.**
> *I have an (older) sister. ("An older sister exists.")*
>
> 娘がいます。 **musume ga imasu.**
> *I have a daughter.*
>
> 弟はいません。 **otouto wa imasen.**
> *I don't have a younger brother.*

What does it mean?

Join the English to the pronunciation and the Japanese script, as in the example.

English	Pronunciation	Japanese
children	oniisan	お父さん
my husband	otouto	奥さん
older brother	kodomo	お姉さん
my daughter	chichi	息子さん
father	goshujin	ご主人
my mother	musukosan	お兄さん
older sister	imoutosan	妹さん
my younger brother	otousan	子供
wife	otto	父
husband	musume	弟
younger sister	haha	娘
son	okusan	母
my father	oneesan	夫

Language Focus

You have seen that when talking about your own family the concept of *my* is communicated within the word itself and there is no need for a separate word to express possession. Similarly, when addressing someone else about their family you would not need a separate word for *your:*

> ロバートさん、弟さんがいますか。
> **robaato san, otoutosan ga imasu ka?** *Robert, do you have a younger brother?*
>
> はい、弟がいます。
> **hai, otouto ga imasu.** *Yes, I have a younger brother.*
>
> 弟さんの名前は何ですか。
> **otoutosan no namae wa nan desu ka?** *What's your younger brother's name?*
>
> 弟の名前はピーターです。
> **otouto no namae wa piitaa desu.** *My younger brother's name is Peter.*

Now look again at the last two sentences. Here we can see examples of how other possessives are formed in Japanese. The particle の **no** between 弟さん **otoutosan** and 名前 **namae** is the equivalent of the English *'s* as in *Jane's pen* and is used to express possession.

When の **no** is used together with the word for *I* the meaning becomes *my:*

> 私のペン
> **watashi no pen** *my pen*
>
> 私の車は小さいです。
> **watashi no kuruma wa chiisai desu.** *My car is small.*

Remember that when expressing *your, his, her,* etc., Japanese prefers to use people's names rather than pronouns.

> 安紀子さんの猫は大きいです。
> **akiko san no neko wa ookii desu.** *Her (Akiko's) cat is big.*
>
> 優子さんのコンピュータは小さいですね。
> **yuuko san no konpyuuta wa chiisai desu ne.** *Yuuko, your computer is small, isn't it?*

If we wish to use a possessive to say that something or someone belongs to something or someone else then we would combine **の no** with the structure we learned earlier, **...は ...です** *...wa ...desu.*

> ピーターさんはロバートさんのお兄さんです。
> **piitaa san wa robaato san no oniisan desu.**
> *Peter is Robert's older brother.*

Family Tree

Make up sentences about this family, as in the example.
Don't forget to use the words for talking about someone else's family

優子さんは実さんの妹さんです。

yuuko san wa minoru san no imoutosan desu.

Yuuko is Minoru's younger sister.

正   安紀子

実   優子

Robert's family

Listen to Robert answering questions about his family.
Circle the correct names on the family tree, as in the example.

35

ピーター
ケン
マーク

セーラ
ヘレン
メリー

ロバート
ケン
ピーター

ロバート
マーク
ピーター

Questions and answers

Now read the questions on the left and then match them to the answers on the right that Robert gave, as in the example.

お名前は？

ご兄弟がいますか。

お母さんの名前は何ですか。

お兄さんの名前は何ですか。

お父さんの名前は何ですか。

どこから来ましたか。

ロンドンから来ました。

父の名前はケンです。

兄がいます。

ロバートです。

母の名前はヘレンです。

兄の名前はピーターです。

Language Focus

A useful phrase for introducing people is:

> こちらは ... さんです。
> **kochira wa ... san desu.** *This is ...*

However, if you are introducing a member of your own family you do not need to say こちらは kochira wa. You can also omit さん san after the name:

> 妹のセーラです。
> **imouto no Seera desu.** *This is my younger sister Sarah.*

Don't forget to add さん san after the person's name if they are not a member of your own family, as a sign of respect.

> – セーラさん, こんにちは。
> **seera san konnichiwa.** *Hello, Sarah.*
>
> – メリーさん, こんにちは。
> **merii san konnichiwa.** *Hello, Mary.*
>
> – 兄のマークです。
> **ani no maaku desu.** *This is my (older) brother, Mark.*
>
> – はじめまして、マークさん。セーラです。
> **hajimemashite, maaku san. seera desu.**
> *Pleased to meet you, Mark. I'm Sarah.*
>
> – はじめまして、セーラさん。
> **hajimemashite, seera san.** *Pleased to meet you, Sarah.*

Now introduce *your* family. Follow the prompts on your audio CD.

36

 *Key Words*

一	ichi	*one*	六	roku	*six*
二	ni	*two*	七	nana/shichi	*seven*
三	san	*three*	八	hachi	*eight*
四	shi/yon	*four*	九	kyu/ku	*nine*
五	go	*five*	十	juu	*ten*

 Language Focus

The numbers listed above are those which would be used for counting on your fingers and for doing arithmetic. To make higher numbers we simply combine the numbers 1 to 10. For example 11 (10 + 1) = 十一 **juuichi**, 20 (2 x 10) = 二十 **nijuu**, 52 (5 x 10 + 2) = 五十二 **gojuuni**. The second pronunciation for *four* and *seven* is used in combinations, e.g. 40 = 四十 **yonjuu** (*not* **shijuu**).

To count things in Japanese is more complicated. We cannot use only this set of numbers. Everything counted also needs a "classifier." The classifier is put after the number.

For example, the classifier for counting people (including family members) is 人 **nin**, which we met when talking about nationality. Here is how to count people up to 10. Notice the special pronunciation for *1 person* and *2 people*:

一人	**hitori**	*1 person*	六人	**rokunin**	*6 people*
二人	**futari**	*2 people*	七人	**shichinin**	*7 people*
三人	**sannin**	*3 people*	八人	**hachinin**	*8 people*
四人	**yonin**	*4 people*	九人	**kyuunin**	*9 people*
五人	**gonin**	*5 people*	十人	**juunin**	*10 people*

How many?

Match the numbers with the figures, as in the example.

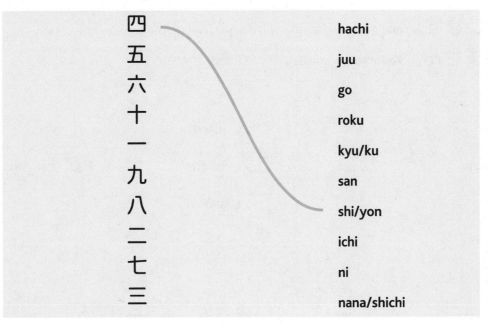

四
五
六
十
一
九
八
二
七
三

hachi

juu

go

roku

kyu/ku

san

shi/yon

ichi

ni

nana/shichi

Japanese sums

Circle the correct answer to these sums, as in the example.

1 一 + 三 = 一、二、三、④、五、六、七、八、九、十
2 四 + 二 = 一、二、三、四、五、六、七、八、九、十
3 二 x 三 = 一、二、三、四、五、六、七、八、九、十
4 五 + 三 = 一、二、三、四、五、六、七、八、九、十
5 六 - 二 = 一、二、三、四、五、六、七、八、九、十
6 七 + 三 = 一、二、三、四、五、六、七、八、九、十
7 九 - 四 = 一、二、三、四、五、六、七、八、九、十
8 八 + 一 = 一、二、三、四、五、六、七、八、九、十
9 六 - 五 = 一、二、三、四、五、六、七、八、九、十

My family

Use the table below to make sentences about yourself, as in the examples.

姉が二人います。 **ane ga futari imasu.** *I have two (older) sisters.*

子供はいません。 **kodomo wa imasen.** *I don't have any children.*

姉 ane		一人 hitori	
妹 imouto	が ga	二人 futari	います。 imasu.
兄 ani		三人 sannin	
弟 otouto			
息子 musuko			
娘 musume	は wa	いません。 imasen.	
子供 kodomo			

Listen and speak

38

Now imagine you are with some of your family looking for the station and you meet a Japanese friend.

Carefully prepare the information below that you will need to take part in the conversation. Then go to your audio CD and see how you get on introducing your family.

1 Think of two members of your family – one male and one female. For example, your husband and your daughter; or your brother and your mother.

2 How would you tell someone their names in Japanese?

3 How would you ask *Where is the station?*

4 How do you say *thank you* and *goodbye?*

You can repeat the conversation, but this time use two different members of your family and ask how to get to the bus stop.

 **Bingo!**

1 Cut out the small number tokens and the bingo cards on Game Card 7.

2 Find 16 buttons for each player or make 16 small blank pieces of card (to cover the squares on the bingo card).

3 Put the tokens into a bag and shake thoroughly.

4 Pull out a number token and say the number out loud in Japanese.

5 If you have that number on your card, cover the square with a button or blank piece of card. If you have more than one square with that number, you can only cover one.

6 Put the number token back in the bag and shake again.

7 Repeat steps 3–6 until you have all the squares covered on the bingo card. Then you can shout:
ヤッタ **yatta!** *I've won!*

You can play with a friend or challenge yourself.

GAME CARD **7** (see page 73)

十	七	五	一
一	九	九	七
六	八	三	四
二	五	四	一

四	八	一	八
十	二	九	六
三	八	三	七
六	十	二	五

一
二
三
四
五
六
七
八
九
十

 ## Key Words

39

先生 **sensei**	*teacher*		運転手 **untenshu**	*driver*	
学生 **gakusei**	*student*		コック **kokku**	*cook/chef*	
医者 **isha**	*doctor*		俳優 **haiyuu**	*actor*	
サラリーマン **sarariiman**	*office worker*		技師 **gishi**	*engineer*	
店員 **ten'in**	*store assistant*		会計士 **kaikeishi**	*accountant*	

If your occupation or those of your family aren't listed here, try to find out what they are in Japanese.

What does it mean?

Join the Japanese to the pronunciation and the English, as in the example.

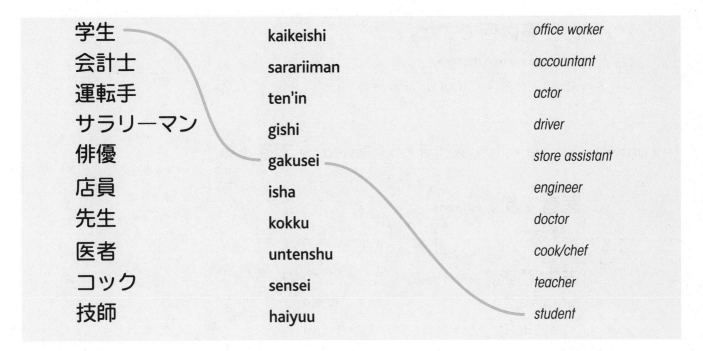

学生	kaikeishi	office worker
会計士	sarariiman	accountant
運転手	ten'in	actor
サラリーマン	gishi	driver
俳優	gakusei	store assistant
店員	isha	engineer
先生	kokku	doctor
医者	untenshu	cook/chef
コック	sensei	teacher
技師	haiyuu	student

The tools of the trade

Match the jobs to the tools of the trade, as in the example.

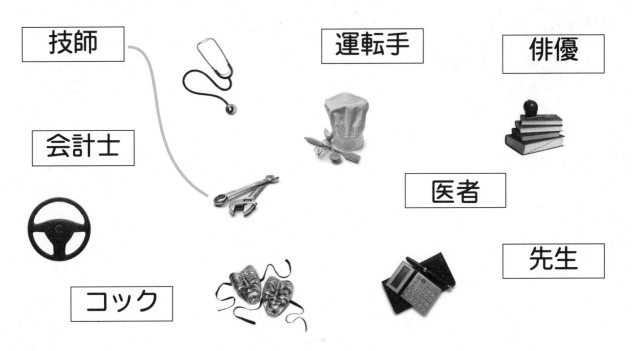

技師

運転手

俳優

会計士

医者

コック

先生

 *Language Focus*

To ask someone what they do for a living, use the following question:

お仕事は何ですか。

oshigoto wa nan desu ka.

What's your job? ("As for job, what is it?")

The answer is simple – just give the job followed by です **desu.**

医者です。 **isha desu.**

I'm a doctor.

先生です。 **sensei desu.**

I'm a teacher.

Other possible answers include:

退職しました。 **taishoku shimashita.**

I'm retired.

働いていません。 **hataraiteimasen.**

I'm not working at the moment.

40

Listen and note

Listen to two people telling you about themselves and fill out the details in English on the forms below. (Note that 家族 **kazoku** means *family*, and ご家族 **gokazoku** is the polite way to refer to someone else's family.)

Name: ...... *Akiko* ....

Family name: ....

Nationality: ....

Name of spouse: ....

No. of children: ....

Occupation: ....

Name: ....

Family name: ....

Nationality: ....

Name of spouse: ....

No. of children: ....

Occupation: ....

Your turn to speak

41

Now you give the same information about yourself.
Follow the prompts on your audio CD.

What's the answer?

Match the questions to the answers.

For example: **1d**

1 お名前は何ですか。

2 どこから来ましたか。

3 奥さんの名前は何ですか。

4 お子さんがいますか。

5 お仕事は何ですか。

a 息子が一人と娘が二人います。

b 俳優です。

c オーストラリアから来ました。

d ハリーです。

e 妻の名前はジュリーです。

Which word?

Write the correct number of the word in the box to complete the description, as in the example.

1 子供　**2** 娘　**3** 俳優　**4** 妻

5 一人　**6** です　**7** オーストラリア

ハリーです。_3_です。

___ のメルボーンから来ました。

___ の名前はジュリー___。

___ が三人います。息子が ___

と___ が二人います。

 # Key Words

42

工場 **koujou**	*factory*		事務所 **jimusho**		*office*
病院 **byouin**	*hospital*		大学 **daigaku**		*college/ university*
店 **mise**	*store*				
劇場 **gekijou**	*theater*		*Look back as well at the Key Words on page 54 for other places of work.*		

 # Language Focus

勤めています tsutometeimasu (*to work*) can be used together with the particle に ni to say *where* you work. The work place comes first in the sentence:

> 医者です。病院に勤めています。
>
> **isha desu. byouin ni tsutometeimasu.**
>
> *I'm a doctor. I work in a hospital.*

We can be more specific about where we work by adding a town or city. Notice the use of the particle の no to link the town/city and the place of work:

> 医者です。大阪の病院に勤めています。
>
> **isha desu. oosaka no byouin ni tsutometeimasu.**
>
> *I am a doctor. I work in a hospital in Osaka.*

To ask where someone works you would say:

> どこに勤めていますか。
>
> **doko ni tsutometeimasu ka.** *Where do you work?*

Word Square

Can you find the 8 different work places in the word square?
Words can read horizontally or vertically.
Write out the meaning for the words you have found.

事	工	場	ソ	テ	ー	ブ	ル
か	ば	ん	ス	病	髪	場	ン
さ	公	で	さ	院	園	車	場
お	店	空	劇	場	レ	銀	行
こ	大	学	ピ	ュ	ス	タ	あ
レ	ー	毛	い	腹	ト	事	そ
ト	院	誌	う	の	ラ	務	こ
ソ	フ	ァ	ー	場	ン	所	シ

factory _____

_____

_____

_____

_____

_____

_____

Now make sentences for each of the work places, as in the example:

技師です。工場に勤めています。

gishi desu. koujou ni tsutometeimasu.

I'm an engineer. I work in a factory.

What are they saying?

Match the people with what they are saying. For example: **1e**

1 東京のレストランに勤めています。

2 イギリスの学校に勤めています。

3 アメリカの銀行に勤めています。

4 大阪の店に勤めています。

5 俳優です。

6 カナダの工場に勤めています。

a

b

c

d

e

f

Listen and speak

Imagine you are a chef. You're meeting someone for the first time and they are asking you about yourself.

43

Carefully prepare the information below that you will need to take part in the conversation. Then go to your audio CD and see how you get on talking about yourself.

1 Your name is Minoru (実).

2 You're from Tokyo.

3 You're a chef.

4 You work in a Japanese restaurant in New York.

5 You have two daughters.

6 Your wife is a teacher in a big school.

Which word?

Now write the correct number of the word in the box to complete the description of Minoru's life, as in the example.

> **1** 勤めています　**2** 四人　**3** から　**4** 娘
>
> **5** 学生　**6** 先生　**7** レストラン　　**8** 学校

はじめまして。実です。東京 *3* 来ました。コックです。

ニューヨークの ___ に ___ 。家族とニューヨークに住んでいます

sundeimasu *(to live)*。___ 家族です。妻と ___ が二人います。妻は ___ です。

レストランのとなりに日本の学校があります。この ___ に勤めています。

娘はニューヨーク大学の ___ です。

Where do I work?

① Tear out the work-place picture cards and profession word cards on Game Card 8.

② Turn the cards face down on a table, with the pictures on one end of the table and the words on the other.

③ Turn over a word card and say ...です ... desu (*I'm a ...*) as appropriate, e.g.:

先生です。 **sensei desu.** *I'm a teacher.*

④ Then turn over a picture card. If the work-place picture matches the profession, say ...に勤めています ...**ni tsutometeimasu** (*I work in a/an...*), e.g.:

学校に勤めています。 **gakkou ni tsutometeimasu.** *I work in a school.*

⑤ If you turn over a matching picture and say both sentences correctly you get to keep the cards. If you don't, you must turn the cards face down and try again.

⑥ The winner is the one who collects the most cards.

⑦ You can compete with a friend or challenge yourself against the clock.

(Review the vocabulary on pages 54, 56 and 74 before you play the game.)

GAME CARD 8 (see page 83)

Picture cards:

Profession cards:

先生	学生	医者	サラリーマン
運転手	コック	俳優	技師
会計士	店員		

先生

This *Test Yourself* section reviews all the Japanese you have learned in this program. Have a go at the activities. If you find you have forgotten something, go back to the relevant topic(s) and look again at the *Key Words* and *Language Focus* panels.

May I have...?

Ask for the following, as in the example:

black

紅茶をお願いします。 koocha o onegaishimasu.

1

4

2
green

5

3

6

44

Listen and check

Listen to Akiko talking about herself and decide if the following sentences are true or false.

		True	False
1	Akiko is Japanese.	☐	☐
2	She comes from a small town.	☐	☐
3	She's a teacher.	☐	☐
4	She works in France.	☐	☐
5	Her husband is an engineer.	☐	☐
6	She has five children.	☐	☐

Which word?

Now write the correct number of the word in the box to complete the description of Akiko, as in the example.

1 子供	**2** 大きい	**3** 勤めています	**4** 夫
5 一人	**6** 来ました	**7** 先生	**8** 娘

はじめまして。安紀子です。大阪から__6__。大阪は____市です。

私は____です。イギリスにある日本の学校に____。____は医者です。

日本の学校のとなりに大きい病院があります。夫はこの病院に勤めています。

____が四人います。____が三人と息子が____います。

Can you try and make up a similar description about yourself?

Read and check

Look at the picture and decide if the sentences are true or false.
Look back at topics 4–6 if you are unsure of any of the words.

		True	False
1	銀行があります。	☐	☐
2	銀行の右に病院があります。	☐	☐
3	銀行の左に学校があります。	☐	☐
4	犬がいます。	☐	☐
5	車はありません。	☐	☐
6	車の上に小さい猫がいます。	☐	☐
7	学校の後ろに大きい木があります。	☐	☐
8	病院の前に古い自転車があります。	☐	☐

What does it mean?

Can you remember these words? Join the words and write the pronunciation next to the Japanese, as in the example

children	息子	*musuko*
my husband	父	
my son	母	
my daughter	妹	
my father	兄	
my mother	姉	
my younger sister	子供	
my older brother	夫	
my older sister	娘	
my wife	弟	
my younger brother	妻	

How do you say it?

Now see if you can say these in Japanese, as in the example.

1 My husband is a doctor.
夫は医者です。
otto wa isha desu.

2 I have a younger sister.

3 Our son is an engineer.

4 Minoru is Yuuko's older brother.

5 My wife's name is Sarah.

6 Her younger brother is an actor.

7 I don't have any children.

8 I have three daughters.

At the tourist office

45

Finally, you are going to test your new Japanese conversational skills by joining in the dialog on your audio CD.

You're going to ask for some information at a tourist information office.

To prepare, first see if you can remember these words and phrases. Write the pronunciation and English next to the Japanese, as in the example.

さようなら	*sayounara goodbye*
博物館	_____
バス停	_____
左に曲がって下さい	_____
おはようございます	_____
どこ	_____
後ろ	_____
ありがとうございます	_____
上	_____
駅	_____

Now follow the prompts on your audio CD. Don't worry if you don't manage everything the first time around. Just keep repeating it until you are fluent.

Congratulations on successfully completing this introductory *Read & Speak Japanese* program. You have overcome the obstacle of learning an unfamiliar language and a different script. You should now have the confidence to enjoy using the Japanese you have learned. You have also acquired a sound basis from which to expand your language skills in whichever direction you choose. Good luck!

This *Reference* section gives an overview of the Japanese script and pronunciation. You can use it to refer to as you work your way through the *Read & Speak Japanese* program. Don't expect to take it all in from the beginning. *Read & Speak Japanese* is designed to build your confidence step by step as you progress through the topics. The details will start to fall into place gradually as you become more familiar with the Japanese characters and language.

The Japanese script

No one can pretend that the Japanese writing system is simple. For historic reasons, the Japanese language is written in a combination of three different writing systems: *kanji*, the Chinese system of ideograms adopted by Japanese; *hiragana*, a script used mainly for words of Japanese origin; and *katakana*, a script used to write foreign loan words, of which there are many.

Although it is possible to write all words in katakana, and indeed this is how Japanese children first learn to write, there is a commonly accepted way of writing a particular word and this is one you would see in everyday life. This program presents the words and phrases as they are normally written.

Kanji (Chinese Characters)

Kanji is not an alphabet, but a series of ideograms, or characters. These characters originally evolved in China from pictograms and the writing system was later adopted by the Japanese. A few characters still resemble the object or concept they refer to, but most have changed beyond recognition.

Japanese uses kanji to write basic words and concepts. Most words connected with the natural world or universal concepts, such as **big** and **cat**, will be represented by kanji, or a combination of kanji with added hiragana.

Some words consist of a single kanji, others are made up of two or more characters:

家	ie *house*	学校	gakkou *school*
猫	neko *cat*	運転手	untenshu *driver*

There is no way of working out the pronunciation of kanji. You will need to learn them on an individual basis.

Katakana and Hiragana

Although often referred to as an *alphabets*, katakana and hiragana are actually *syllabaries*. Each character represents a syllable (a consonant plus a vowel), such as **ha** or **fu**. You will find the katakana and hiragana syllabaries opposite, but do not try to learn them by heart. It is better to give these tables a quick glance and then move on to the topics. As you meet each word or phrase, you can refer to the tables if you want to work out the individual characters.

The signs **"** and **°** are used to add further sounds to the characters in the tables. In addition, a long dash (ー) is used to lengthen a sound in some katakana words. For example, the katakana character テ **te** is lengthened to テー **tee** by adding this dash:

> テーブル **teeberu** *table*
> セーラ **seera** *Sarah*

Hiragana is sometimes used to write complete words:

> こんにちは **konnichiwa** *hello*
> そば **soba** *noodles*

But many others are made up of a kanji ideogram with a hiragana ending:

> 古い **furui** *old*
> 後ろ **ushiro** *behind*

The structural words and grammatical particles which "glue" the language together tend to be written in hiragana, for example です **desu** (*am/is/are*), は **wa** (topic marker "*as for*"), and か **ka** (*question marker*). Watching out for these will help you to break up sentences and questions into their component parts:

> お名前は何ですか。 **onamae wa nan desu ka?**
> *What is your name? ("name as for what is it")*

Hiragana Syllabary

あ a	か ka	さ sa	た ta	な na	は ha	ま ma	や ya	ら ra	わ wa
い i	き ki	し shi	ち chi	に ni	ひ hi	み mi		れ ri	
う u	く ku	す su	つ tsu	ぬ nu	ふ fu	む mu	ゆ yu	る ru	
え e	け ke	せ se	て te	ね ne	へ he	め me		れ re	
お o	こ ko	そ so	と to	の no	ほ ho	も mo	よ yo	ろ ro	を (w)o
				ん n					

Katakana Syllabary

ア a	カ ka	サ sa	タ ta	ナ na	ハ ha	マ ma	ヤ ya	ラ ra	ワ wa
イ i	キ ki	シ shi	チ chi	ニ ni	ヒ hi	ミ mi		リ ri	
ウ u	ク ku	ス su	ツ tsu	ヌ nu	フ fu	ム mu	ユ yu	ル ru	
エ e	ケ ke	セ se	テ te	ネ ne	ヘ he	メ me		レ re	
オ o	コ ko	ソ so	ト to	ノ no	ホ ho	モ mo	ヨ yo	ロ ro	ヲ wo
				ン n					

Pronunciation

The syllables in Japanese are pronounced equally and there is no particular emphasis on any part of the word. Many letters are pronounced in a similar way to English, but look out for these more unfamiliar sounds:

f   a Japanese f is pronounced without putting your lower teeth over your upper lip

r   somewhere between the English *r* and *l*

w   pronounced with slack rather than rounded lips

You will find an introduction to the sounds of Japanese on track 1 of your audio CD.

ANSWERS

Topic 1

Page 6
Check your answers with the Key Words panel on page 5.

Page 8: What are they saying?

Page 8: What do you hear?
You should have checked boxes 2 and 5.

Page 10: What does it mean?
1a, 2f, 3e, 4b, 5d, 6c

Page 10: Which word?

おはよう___2___.

___5___ ございます。

安紀子___4___ 。お名前___3___ 。

___1___ です。

Page 11: What are their names?

セーラ	seera	Sarah	ピーター	piittaa	Peter
ヘレン	heren	Helen	ケン	ken	Ken
メリー	merii	Mary	マーク	maaku	Mark
リサ	risa	Lisa	ロバート	robaato	Robert
ハナ	hana	Hannah	ジェームス	jeemusu	James

Page 12: In or out?
IN: Sarah, Minoru, Yuuko, Ken, Tadashi
OUT: James, Robert, Akiko, Helen, Mary

Topic 2

Page 15: Where are the countries?

カナダ 1　イギリス 4　　日本 6　　　オーストラリア 8

韓国 7　　アイルランド 3　アメリカ 2　中国 5

Page 16: How do you say it?
Check your answers with the Key Words panel on page 14.

Page 16: Where are the cities?
東京は日本にあります。 **toukyou wa nihon ni arimasu.**
大阪は日本にあります。 **oosaka wa nihon ni arimasu.**
ニューヨークはアメリカにあります。
nyuuyooku wa amerika ni arimasu.
シドニーはオーストラリアにあります。
shidonii wa oosutoraria ni arimasu.
ワシントンはアメリカにあります。
washinton wa amerika ni arimasu.
ロンドンはイギリスにあります。
rondon wa igirisu ni arimasu.
ロサンジェルスはアメリカにあります。
rosanjerusu wa amerika ni arimasu.
ダブリンはアイルランドにあります。
daburin wa airurando ni arimasu.

Page 17: Audio track 8
Akiko: Japan; Mary: Australia; Sarah: England; Ken: China

Page 18: Where are they from?

安紀子　　　　　　　　イギリス
メリー　　　　　　　　中国
セーラ　　　　　　　　オーストラリア
ケン　　　　　　　　　日本

Page 20: Who's from where?

1 ピーターさんはアメリカ人です。
　 piittaa san wa amerikajin desu.

2 安紀子さんは日本人です。 akiko san wa nihonjin desu.

3 リサさんはカナダ人です。 risa san wa kanadajin desu.

4 マークさんはオーストラリア人です。
　 maaku san wa oosutorariajin desu.

5 ジェームスさんはアイルランド人です。
　 jeemusu san wa airurandojin desu.

6 スンさんは韓国人です。 **sun san wa kankokujin desu.**

7 実さんは日本人です。 **minoru san wa nihonjin desu.**

8 メリーさんはイギリス人です。 **merii san wa igirisujin desu.**

Page 21: Listen and Check

1 False; 2 True; 3 False; 4 True; 5 False

Page 21: What does it mean?

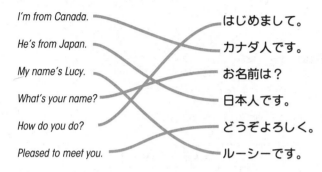

I'm from Canada.	はじめまして。
He's from Japan.	カナダ人です。
My name's Lucy.	お名前は？
What's your name?	日本人です。
How do you do?	どうぞよろしく。
Pleased to meet you.	ルーシーです。

Page 22: What does it mean?

1 ルーシーです。 I'm Lucy.

2 カナダ人です。 I'm Canadian.

3 優子さんは日本人です。 Yuuko is Japanese.

4 お名前は？ What's your name?

5 安紀子です。 I'm Akiko.

6 ピーターさんは何人ですか。 What nationality is Peter?
or Peter, what nationality are you?

7 ジェームスさんはイギリス人です。 James is English.

8 アメリカ人です。 I'm American.

Topic 3

Page 25

Check your answers with the Key Words panel on page 24.

Page 26: Word Square

computer, sofa, bag, magazine, book, chair, television, table

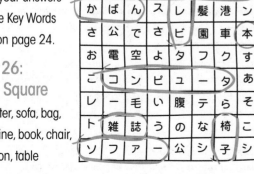

Page 26: Odd One Out

椅子 ＊ テーブル ＊ お名前 ＊ ソファー

電話 ＊ 日本 ＊ アメリカ ＊ 韓国

安紀子 ＊ ペン ＊ ロバート ＊ セーラ

かばん ＊ こんばんは ＊ さようなら ＊ こんにちは

何 ＊ か ＊ どこ ＊ ドア

Page 28: What's this?

1e, 2b, 3f, 4c, 5h, 6d, 7a, 8g

Page 30: Who orders what?

Customer 1: coffee & cake; **Customer 2:** black tea & sandwich

Customer 3: coffee & noodles; **Customer 4:** coffee & cake;

Customer 5: black tea & pork cutlet

Page 31: Unscramble the conversation

g, a, e, c, f, h, d, b

Topic 4

Page 35: What does it mean?

Check your answers with the Key Words panel on page 34.

Page 35: What can you see?

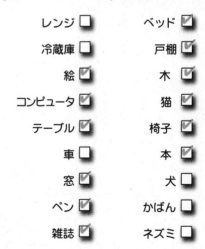

レンジ ☐	ベッド ☑
冷蔵庫 ☐	戸棚 ☑
絵 ☑	木 ☑
コンピュータ ☑	猫 ☑
テーブル ☑	椅子 ☑
車 ☐	本 ☑
窓 ☑	犬 ☐
ペン ☑	かばん ☐
雑誌 ☑	ネズミ ☐

Page 37: Which word?

1 前 2 下 3 上 4 上

5 となり 6 下 7 中

Page 39: Where are the mice?

There are many possible sentences.

If you can, check yours with a native speaker.

Page 41: True or False?

1 True; **2** False; **3** False; **4** True; **5** True; **6** True; **7** False;
8 True; **9** True **10** True

Topic 5

Page 45: Can you remember?

Check your answers with the Key Words panel on page 44.

Page 46: What does it mean?

新しいソファー	(a) new sofa
小さいコーヒー	(a) small coffee
小さい犬	(a) small dog
とても古い車	(a) very old car
小さいネズミ	(a) small mouse
大きいサンドイッチ	(a) big sandwich
安い絵	(an) inexpensive picture
大きい木	big trees

Page 47: Listen and check

1 False; **2** True; **3** True; **4** False; **5** True

Page 47: Unscramble the sentences

1 c, a, b; **2** c, b, e, d, a; **3** c, d, a, b; **4** b, d, c, a

Page 50: Which word?

1 頭 **2** 足 **3** お腹 **4** 口 **5** 指 **6** 髪の毛
7 耳 **8** 鼻 **9** 目 **10** 腕

Page 51: At the pet show

この猫は毛が ___6___ です。足も長い ___2___ 。
___1___ が小さいです。

この犬 ___4___ 毛が短いです。___3___ がとても
小さいです。口が ___5___ です。

Page 52: What does it look like?

There are many possible sentences.

If you can, check yours with a native speaker.

Topic 6

Page 55: Questions and answers

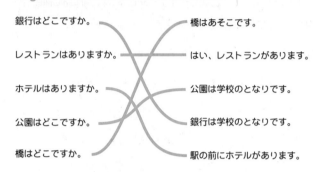

銀行はどこですか。 — 橋はあそこです。
レストランはありますか。 — はい、レストランがあります。
ホテルはありますか。 — 公園は学校のとなりです。
公園はどこですか。 — 銀行は学校のとなりです。
橋はどこですか。 — 駅の前にホテルがあります。

Page 57: Word Square

car, boat, taxi, plane, bicycle, bus, train

駅	船	ラ	ソ	飛	行	機	ル
か	ば	ん	ス	レ	髪	港	ン
バ	公	で	さ	ビ	園	電	車
ー	タ	ク	シ	ー	フ	ク	す
こ	コ	ン	ピ	ュ	ー	タ	あ
レ	ー	毛	い	腹	テ	ら	そ
ト	バ	ス	う	の	な	車	こ
道	フ	ァ	自	転	車	子	シ

Page 60: Which way?

1 すみません、バス停はどこですか。
まっすぐ行って下さい。
sumimasen, basutei wa doko desu ka? massugu itte kudasai.

2 すみません、駅はどこですか。
右に曲がって下さい。
sumimasen, eki wa doko desu ka? migi ni magatte kudasai.

3 すみません、銀行はどこですか。
左に曲がって下さい。
sumimasen, ginkou wa doko desu ka? hidari ni magatte kudasai.

4 すみません、ホテルはどこですか。
まっすぐ行って下さい。
それから右に曲がって下さい。 sumimasen, hoteru wa doko
desu ka? massugu itte kudasai. sore kara migi ni magatte kudasai.

5 すみません、博物館はどこですか。
バスで行きます。 sumimasen, hakubutsukan wa doko desu ka?
basu de ikimasu.

6 すみません、空港はどこですか。電車で行きます。
sumimasen, kuukou wa doko desu ka? densha de ikimasu.

Page 61: Around town

These are model answers. Yours may vary slightly.

the hospital

まっすぐ行って下さい。それから右に曲がって下さい。
病院は銀行のとなりです。 massugu itte kudasai. sore kara migi ni magatte kudasai. byouin wa ginkou no tonari desu.

the park

まっすぐ行って下さい。それから左に曲がって下さい。
公園は学校のとなりです。 massugu itte kudasai. sore kara hidari ni magatte kudasai. kouen wa gakkou no tonari desu.

the bus stop

まっすぐ行って下さい。それから左に曲がって下さい。
バス停は学校の前です。 massugu itte kudasai. sore kara hidari ni magatte kudasai. basutei wa gakkou no mae desu.

Page 62: Unscramble the conversation

e, c, a, b, d

Page 63: Game

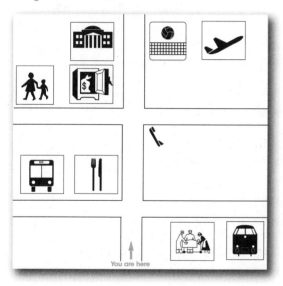

Topic 7

Page 65: What does it mean?

Check your answers with the Key Words panel on page 64.

Page 67: Family Tree

There are many possible sentences.

If you can, check yours with a native speaker.

Page 68: Robert's family

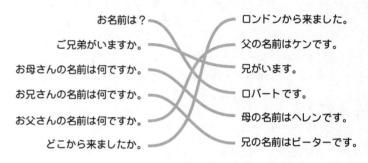

Page 68: Questions and answers

お名前は？ — ロンドンから来ました。
ご兄弟がいますか。 — 父の名前はケンです。
お母さんの名前は何ですか。 — 兄がいます。
お兄さんの名前は何ですか。 — ロバートです。
お父さんの名前は何ですか。 — 母の名前はヘレンです。
どこから来ましたか。 — 兄の名前はピーターです。

Page 71: How many?

四 — hachi
五 — juu
六 — go
十 — roku
一 — kyu/ku
九 — san
八 — shi/yon
二 — ichi
七 — ni
三 — nana/shichi

Page 71: Japanese sums

1 四　2 六　3 六　4 八　5 四
6 十　7 五　8 九　9 一

Topic 8

Page 75: What does it mean?

Check your answers with the Key Words panel on page 74.

Page 75: The tools of the trade

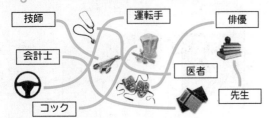

Page 77: Listen and note

1 *First name:* Akiko; *Family name:* Maruyama; *Nationality:* Japanese; *Spouse:* Shouji; *Children:* 2; *Occupation:* teacher
2 *First name:* Peter; *Family name:* Smith; *Nationality:* Irish; *Spouse:* Hannah; *Children:* 1; *Occupation:* accountant

Page 78: What's the answer?

1d, 2c, 3e, 4a, 5b

Page 78: Which word?

ハリーです。　3　です。

7　のメルボーンから来ました。

4　の名前はジュリー　6　。

1　が三人います。息子が　5

と　2　が二人います。

Page 80: Word Square

factory; college; bank; theater; store; restaurant; hospital; office

事	工	場	ソ	テ	ー	ブ	ル
か	ば	ん	ス	病	髪	場	ン
さ	公	で	さ	院	園	車	場
お	店	空	劇	場	レ	銀	行
こ	大	学	ビ	ュ	ス	タ	あ
レ	ー	毛	い	腹	ト	事	そ
ト	院	誌	う	の	ら	務	こ
ソ	フ	ァ	ー	場	ン	所	シ

Page 81: What are they saying?

1e, 2d, 3b, 4c, 5a, 6f

Page 82: Which word?

はじめまして。実です。東京　3　来ました。コックです。
ニューヨークの　7　に　1　。家族とニューヨークに住んでい
ます。　2　家族です。妻と　4　が二人います。妻は　6　です。
レストランのとなりに日本の学校があります。この　8　に勤
めています。娘はニューヨーク大学の　5　です。

Test Yourself

Page 84: May I have…?

Use をお願いします *...o onegaishimasu* with the following:

1コーヒー *koohi*; 2お茶 *ocha*; 3ケーキ *keeki*;
4そば *soba*; 5豚カツ *tonkatsu*; 6サンドイッチ
sandoicchi

Page 85: Listen and check

1 True; 2 False; 3 True; 4 False; 5 False; 6 False

Page 85: Which word?

はじめまして。安紀子です。大阪から　6　。
大阪は　2　市です。私は　7　です。イギリスに
ある日本の学校に　3　。　4　は医者です。
日本の学校のとなりに大きい病院があり
ます。夫はこの病院に勤めています。
1　が四人います。　8　が三人と息子が　5　います。

Page 86: Read and check

1 True; 2 True; 3 False; 4 True; 5 False; 6 True; 7 True; 8 False

Page 87: Read and check

Check your answers with the Key Words panel on page 64.

Page 87: How do you say it?

1 夫は医者です。　*otto wa isha desu.*
2 妹がいます。　*imouto ga imasu.*
3 息子は技師です。　*musuko wa gishi desu.*
4 実さんは優子さんのお兄さんです。
　minoru san wa yuuko san no oniisan desu.
5 妻の名前はセーラです。　*tsuma no namae wa seera desu.*
6 弟さんは俳優です。　*otoutosan wa haiyuu desu.*
7 子供はいません。　*kodomo wa imasen.*
8 娘が三人います。　*musume ga sannin imasu.*

Page 88: At the tourist office

さようなら *sayounara* *goodbye*
博物館 *hakubutsukan* *museum*
バス停 *basutei* *bus stop*
左に曲がって下さい *hidari ni magatte kudasai* *please turn left*
おはようございます *oyahou gozaimasu* *good morning*
どこ *doko* *where*
後ろ *ushiro* *behind*
ありがとうございます *arigatou gozaimasu* *thank you*
上 *ue* *on top of/above*
駅 *eki* *station*

Name cards:

安紀子	優子	正	実
セーラ	ヘレン	メリー	リサ
ロバート	ピーター	ケン	マーク

Sentence-build cards:

	こんにちは	さようなら	です
さん	何	お名前	か
？	は	ありがとうございます	
。	こんばんは	おはようございます	

Minoru	Tadashi	Yuuko	Akiko
Lisa	Mary	Helen	Sarah
Mark	Ken	Peter	Robert

I am	goodbye	hello	
(question marker)	name	what?	"san" (Mr., Mrs. etc.)
thank you	(topic marker)	?	
good morning	good evening	.	

Picture cards:

green

black

GAME CARD ④ (see page 43)

Cut-out pictures (cut round small pictures)

Sentence-build cards:

中	上	下	前
後ろ	となり	がいます	があります
はいません	はありません	です	か
。	ベッド	テーブル	ソファー
窓	椅子	テレビ	コンピュータ
電話	絵	ネズミ	犬
猫	サンドイッチ	の	に

in front of	**under**	**on**	**in**
there is/are *(inanimate)*	**there is/are** *(animate)*	**next to**	**behind**
question marker	**is/are**	**there isn't/aren't** *(inanimate)*	**there isn't/aren't** *(animate)*
sofa	**table**	**bed**	**.**
computer	**television**	**chair**	**window**
dog	**mouse**	**picture**	**telephone**
particle (ni)	*particle* (no)	**sandwich**	**cat**

Picture cards:

Adjective cards:

大きい	小さい	古い	新しい
長い	短い	高い	安い

Picture cards:

You are here

GAME CARD **7** (see page 73)

十	七	五	一
一	九	九	七
六	八	三	四
二	五	四	一

四	八	一	八
十	二	九	六
三	八	三	七
六	十	二	五

一
二
三
四
五
六
七
八
九
十

Picture cards:

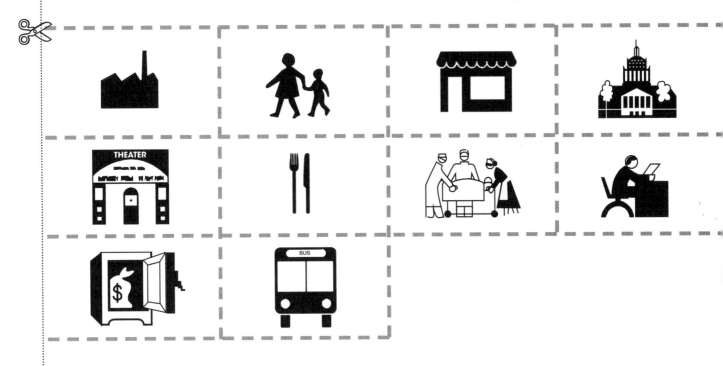

Profession cards:

先生	学生	医者	サラリーマン
運転手	コック	俳優	技師
会計士	店員		